# I Am NOT a Dog

## PET ANIMALS

BY MARI BOLTE

raintree
a Capstone company — publishers for children

Raintree is an imprint of Capstone Global Library Limited, a company incorporated in England and Wales having its registered office at 264 Banbury Road, Oxford, OX2 7DY – Registered company number: 6695582

www.raintree.co.uk
myorders@raintree.co.uk

**Editorial Credits**
Editor: Christianne Jones; Designer: Bobbie Nuytten; Media Researcher: Rebekah Hubstenberger; Production Specialist: Whitney Schaefer

**Image Credits**
Alamy: B.A.E. Inc., 18, 27 (midldle left), Nature Picture Library, 8, 26 (middle left); Dreamstime: Artushfoto, 2-3, Derrick Neill, 22, 27 (bottom left), Pictureguy66, 24, 27 (bottom right); Getty Images: iStock/Julian Parsons, 28, iStock/LPETTET, 10, 26 (middle right), iStock/MikeLane45, 14, 27 (top left), Jaromir Chalabala/EyeEm, 4, 26 (top left), Westend61, 30; Shutterstock: Galyna Andrushko, cover, iusubov nizami, cover (eye), Kristian Bell, 16, 27 (top right), Natalia Golovina, 12, 26 (bottom middle), Nicholas Taffs, 6, 26 (top right), Tracy Wesolek, 20, 27 (middle right), Yevheniia Rodina, design element (desert)

ISBN 978 1 3982 5335 3 (hardback)
ISBN 978 1 3982 5336 0 (paperback)

**British Library Cataloguing in Publication Data**
A full catalogue record for this book is available from the British Library.

Printed and bound in India.

# Who am I?

    People love pets. There are billions of pets cared for in homes around the world. And I am one of them! Owning and caring for a pet has many benefits. We keep people company and make you smile.

    But what animal am I? Read the clues to find out.

I have four legs and use them to follow my nose. My sense of smell is thousands of times better than a human's.

**But I am not a dog.**

I stalk my prey. Then I pounce! Small animals like mice and insects never stand a chance. Then I curl up somewhere warm to rest.

**But I am not a snake.**

People love me because
I am friendly. I come in many
different colours. I need lots of
toys to keep me busy.

**But I am not
a parakeet.**

I am furry and fast! I make noises to let you know how I feel. Sleeping is my favourite hobby. I can nap for 18 to 20 hours a day!

**But I am not a ferret.**

I love finding new places to explore. You may catch a glimpse of my flowing tail as I slink away.

**But I am not a betta fish.**

I'm furry and quiet. I can be sneaky. I'm very independent and often like to be left alone.

**But I am not a tarantula.**

I might look roly-poly, but I can be athletic! I sleep during the day and run around at night.

**But I am not a hedgehog.**

Going somewhere? I love hitching a ride on shoulders. Some people say I look like I'm smiling all the time.

**But I am not a gecko.**

I run fast, and then I fly – or at least leap through the air. You might want to stroke my soft fur. If it's daytime, though, hands off! I need my beauty sleep.

**But I am not a sugar glider.**

I am curious but like to
do things at my own speed.
Growing is one thing I do fast.
My babies get big quickly.

**But I am not
a tortoise.**

Some people think I am a pest. But others think I make a great pet! I keep my home tidy. And I make a happy noise when you stroke me.

**But I am not a rat.**

## I am not a dog

## or a snake

## or a parakeet

## or a ferret

## or a betta fish

**or a tarantula**

**or a hedgehog**

**or a gecko**

**or a sugar glider**

**or a tortoise**

**or a rat.**

## So what animal am I?

# I am a cat!

Cats sleep a lot, pounce and play, and are easy to look after. They are quiet and have soft fur.

There are 11 million pet cats in the UK! Many people own more than one.

# COOL FACTS ABOUT
# CATS

Cats have lived alongside humans for thousands of years. Experts are still not sure when the first cats were domesticated.

Cats have been bred for different physical characteristics, like coat colours or specially shaped ears. But they have not been bred to do different jobs, like dogs.

In 2004, the grave of a pet cat from 9,500 years ago was discovered on the island of Cyprus.

Domestic cats are very similar to their wild relatives who lived thousands of years ago.

Wild cats can have 1 to 8 kittens in one litter. They can have several litters every year.

Nobody knows why cats purr. Happiness and communication are the two most common theories.

# Books in this series

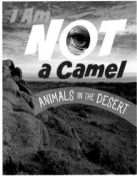

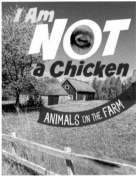

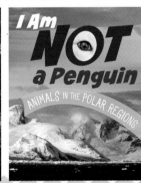

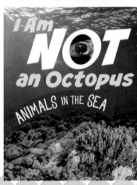

# About the author

Mari Bolte is an author and editor of children's books on all sorts of subjects, from graphic novels about science to art projects to hands-on history. She lives in the middle of a forest full of animals.